—"you have to perceive the[...]
ferent eye, in a different wa[...]
photographers. How you [...]
you take your photos, and [...]
as your subjects—these gi[...]
viduality."—

First published in 1991 by Freezing Speed Publications,
1401 Forty-fifth Street, Studio #1, Emeryville, California
94608 USA.

©John Blakemore, 1989.

ISBN 1-788649-06-X

Freezing Speed is a certified trademark, registered with the
United States Patent Office.

The information in this book is true and complete to the best of
our knowledge. All recommendations are made without any
guarantee on the part of the author and/or publisher, who
disclaim any liability incurred in connection with the use of this
data or specific details.

All photography, text, layout, design and dust cover by John
Blakemore, Berkeley, California, USA.

Printed in the United States of America.

# FREEZING SPEED

## JOHN BLAKEMORE

Preface: Alain Prost

Introduction: Photography and the sport.

1. The Basic Levels: The photographer and his perception.

2. Objectives: What do you want to achieve? The complete story, the practice, the race, the people, the color, the essence of the event, details, cars, atmosphere, mood, weather, action, portraits, or your own special objectives.

3. Planning: Getting to know the circuit, walking the entire circuit, location choice, site selection, light direction, time of day.

4. Film: What kind and why, color, black and white, speed, grain, processing, purchasing, storing, enlarging, projection, special films, bulk loading.

5. Equipment: Cameras, lenses, basic necessary accessories, filters, lights,flash, meters.

6. Composition: Basic theory, good and bad, framing, balance, light and dark, color, movement, dynamics, camera position, camera choice, lens choice.

7. Camera Technique: Shutter speeds, metering, exposure, auto-exposure, programmable cameras, focus, depth of field, pre-focus, follow-focus, action, still, frozen action, peak action, panning, practice.

8. Special Techniques: Zooming, slow shutter speeds, special filters, flash with available light, multiple exposures, success ratio.

9. Adverse Conditions: You and your equipment, rain, wind, sand, heat, cold, film, results.

10. Dangers: Physical risks, you, the drivers, the crowd, your camera, the sport.

11. A Special Eye: Taking a photographic risk, cost vs. results, shot ratio, trying the extraordinary, your perception, your creative difference, lens choice, angle choice, and your choice of subject.

## Preface d'Alain Prost

Ah, les photographes! Je les connais bien, ils font partie si j'ose dire du paysage de la Formule 1 et donc de mon paysage. Les pilotes automobiles ont l'oeil à tout: lorsque, dans une trajectoire, je vise le point de corde du virage avec les roues avant de ma voiture et que j'ai le soleil dans les yeux— je crois que c'est le bon éclairage, la "bonne lumière" comme ils disent—il n'est pas rare que ma vue embrasse la ligne blanche, le rail, et, derrière, quelques objectifs, quelques viseurs dûment pointés. Les photographes sont là, prêts à faire le "doc," celui qui illustrera la couverture d'un magazine, la Une d'un journal sportif, ou la double page d'un beau livre.

Ainsi que certains de mes amis journalistes, pour rire, je donne quelquefois aux photographes le surnom de "techniciens" ou de "ouvriers."Comme si je ne les considérais que comme des "presse-boutons" avec des appareils automatiques, à comparer aux intellectuels. Mais, bien entendu, c'est par humour et surtout par affection. Chez les photographes en effet j'admire le témperament artistique de même que la constance et la détermination. Qu'importe la pluie ou le soleil brûlant, ils sont là, fidèles à leur métier et j'aime çà.

Vous pouvez facilement l'imaginer ma scène préférée avec les photographes, c'est évidemment lá première marche du podium, celle de la victoire. Je perçois des tas de visages connus et souriants, j'entends, derrière les boîtiers et les objectifs, des "Alan, Alène, Alin, Alaine, petit, Prost" et je sais qu'il faut que je regarde les photographes droit dans les yeux pour que la photo du vainqueur soit réussie. Je le fais d'autant plus volontiers que je suis heureux.

Bien sûr, dans le nombre, se glissent de temps à autres quelques paparazzi, qui sont là uniquement pour filmer l'accident et le drame. Mais, depuis que je cours en Formule 1, j'ai remarqué que leur existence était éphémère. Les photographes de Grand Prix ont leurs propres règles, leur propre code et leur propres lois, malheur à qui les transgresse. Ils sont intransigeants sur le chapitre de la pudeur et ainsi est préservé le lien qui unit les vrais professionnels de la F 1: le respect et la complicité.

Alain Prost, 17/2/90

## Foreword: Alain Prost

Ah, photographers! I know them well. They are (if I may say so) part of the scenery of Formula 1, and therefore part of my scenery as well. The drivers notice everything. When in a curve, I aim my front wheels for the perfect apex, the sun in my eyes—I believe that is good lighting (for photography), the "bonne lumiere", as they say—it is not unusual for my view to encompass the white line, the railing and behind it several lenses, several viewfinders properly aimed. The photographers are there ready to take the "shot", to illustrate the cover of a magazine, Page One of a sporting newspaper, or a two page spread in a beautiful book.

As do some of my journalist friends, for fun I sometimes call photographers "technicians" or "robots", as if I considered them nothing more than button-pushers with automatic cameras, as opposed to thinkers. But in reality, I admire photographers' artistic temperament, as well as their persistence and determination. Whether in the pouring rain or the burning sun, they are there, true to their profession, and I like that.

You can easily imagine my favorite pose for the photographers; that is obviously the top step, the winner's spot on the podium. I notice a lot of familiar, smiling faces behind the cameras and lenses, and I hear; "Allon, Alaine, Alan, Aileen, petit Prost", and I know I must look the photographers right in the eye in order to get a good photo of the winner. I do so with pleasure, as it comes easily when I am happy.

## INTRODUCTION:

Since the discovery of the photographic technique, photographers have been trying to freeze action, motion and the essence of action with movement, to record it, to preserve it, to simulate it, in a latent image, on photosensitive materials. From the earliest photographers with the earliest photographic equipment there has been an attempt to capture or freeze speed.

The French were the first to put a price on photographic technique. As early as 1872, the *Societé Francaise de Photographie* offered a prize of 500 French francs to anyone creating a film that would make it possible to stop a street full of moving traffic.

Photography has grown up along with motor racing. Early automobiles were racing and meeting new speed goals, and early cameras were right there to record and "Freeze the Speed." Both have been comfortable partners in the quest for achievement. Technology in motor racing and photography have seen phenomenal growth and incredible sophistication in a very short span of time. But the gauge of how good or how bad the final result is must always come back to the human element. In the case of the Grand Prix driver, it ultimately comes down to the talent of the driver. The same is true for the photographer.

The present cameras and films are designed so that anyone can take photographs; anyone can get a proper exposure, a proper image, and freeze that image. But how well that goal is ac-complished, with good or bad technique, and with how much flair, is in the hand and eye of the photographer. Coordination of the hand and eye is necessary to assure that you have recorded what you have seen, but the eye is the most important. The eye—that is how *you* perceive the subject, how *you* render it— is the key to successful photography.

The Grand Prix, Formula One, is the paramount of motoring sport and the pinnacle of motoring pho-tography. In both, it is the most difficult to work, the most varied, the most competitive and the most exciting. The Grand Prix photographer records only sixteen events per year, but those are usually spread over sixteen different countries and four different continents! This work continues for usu-ally eight months: week after week of attempting to capture something different, meaningful, unique, or explosive; something visually exciting, race after race, week after week, year after year. For those who participate for the full season each year, Grand Prix is truly the highest form of automotive photo-graphic art.

The purpose of this book is to give the viewer, the reader, an opportunity to learn some of the techniques and see some of the possibilities of motor racing photography. This book will deal strictly with the Grand Prix, the Formula One race for the world championship. Other forms of motor racing are exciting in their own fashions, but each in its own way is easier to work, more relaxed, less pressured. The techniques you learn here can be applied to any other form of motoring photography—or, for that matter, to basic photography in general.

Every time I go to a motor race it never ceases to amaze me how many of the spectators have cameras; almost everyone has at least one. Unfortunately, the results for most will be very disappointing. They will be using everything from ancient Instamatics (and even disposable cameras!) to the most sophisticated new, modern, auto-everything electronic marvels that currently pass for cameras. For years, would-be photojournalists and enthusiastic amateurs have approached me and asked how I took a certain photo in this magazine or that, and I would find myself deep in conversation on technique and theory right in the paddock, in the crowd, or oftentimes track-side.

In 1983 I started presenting a limited number of photo seminars, primarily for the Formula One Spectators' Association at various Formula One events. I found that the spectators have a great deal of interest in getting good photographs of the events they attend; the Formula One fan has an unbridled passion for his or her chosen sport and is interested in capturing or preserving that experience in the best way possible. The camera is usually the best way to capture the event and take it home, perhaps to share with others or perhaps just to remember and enjoy. Video might interest some, but it is not permitted in the Formula One pits, paddock, or trackside due to copyright regulations and television rights. This means if you bring your video recorder or movie camera to a Formula One race there is a good chance it will be confiscated by security and the cassette destroyed, and you'll be without a camera for the duration of the weekend!

It is my intent that this book will provide insight into the techniques of Grand Prix photography and also act as an inspiration to view our sport with a new and more creative eye. I hope that at your next race you will be able to see with wider perspective, absorb more detail, and become even more impassioned about the pinnacle of motor racing, the Grand Prix: Formula One.

## CHAPTER 1: BASICS

The basic element of Grand Prix photography is your perception: how you perceive the sport. How you create and record your image of the sport. Your perception gives you your unique creative eye. You see published work all around you; many times, I'll wager, you've said to yourself, "I could have taken a photo as good as that! My photography is better than that!" Or perhaps you had some really great shots you sent off to that magazine, only to have them returned with a polite thank you, but unused.

There is a lot more to this business than just sending a photo off to a magazine, or, for that matter, getting published. Just because a photo is published doesn't mean it is good; often it simply means it got there on time!Conversely, just because it's *not* published doesn't mean it isn't good, either. It could mean the timing was off, the deadline wasn't met, the race was already assigned to another photographer, or other reasons too numerous to mention.

The amateur photographer, the independent photographer, and the freelance photographer have the hardest time getting published because motorsports photography is a very tight and closed market.There are approximately fifty photographers who regularly cover Formula One, doing the majority of the work for most of the world's magazines; out of those there are only about thirty who are able to cover the entire season. That doesn't leave much left for the freelancer or the enlightened amateur.

To get the work, you have to perceive the sport with a different eye, in a different way than the other photographers. How you perceive it, how you take your photos, and what you choose as your subjects—these give you your individuality.

Anyone can take a picture of a car on the track. (Well, okay, sometimes you miss when you're getting started because of poor technique.) It's really simple: Just follow all the other photo books that have a section on action photography. Then, just as they recommend, get "ultra-high-speed" film, use an extremely high shutter speed, and bang,! You've frozen it right there, right on the spot! But does it look like it's moving? Or does it look like the car is stopped, stalled on the track? Not very exciting, is it? Pretty grainy, too! But it did at least record what the car looked like.

Unfortunately, most magazines and many of their art directors don't see much past this point. "The space calls for a shot of the winner. Yep, that's him. It's pretty sharp. The exposure's okay; let's use it. Not much feeling, but it'll have to do. No time to wait for the other film to come in!" A bit exaggerated, at some magazines, but as for others. . . .

For some magazines, it's the use of the stock photo of the stock car on the stock track simply to record the event. There is more junk published than great work. For various reasons, magazines don't always have the luxury of publishing the best photo; sometimes they run the only one they have. Other times the art director just doesn't see a subject the same way the photographer does—or simply doesn't know the sport. A slipshod but all-too-common approach to handling a tight deadline and a difficult sport.

There are, sadly, very few magazines or publications that will give you a full in-depth photographic view of a Formula One Grand Prix. To this end, this book tries to give you some insight, to help you produce better quality photographs, images that are exciting, vivid and imaginative, that can fill the gaps that the magazines and newspapers leave void.

Learn from other photographers' work. Some of it will be great, but on the other hand, some will be lousy. Learn the difference; you can learn from bad photography as well as from good. Just be sure that you learn the difference!

Try not to do what everyone else is doing; try to develop a technique of your own, something that says this is *your* picture, not just a duplicate of someone else's. Your eye is unique in the way it will perceive a subject, so give it a chance to tell its own story with its own creativity.

The primary key to good photographic results is in how you perceive your subject. What is good or pleasing to you may or may not be pleasing to another viewer. Ultimately, you need to please yourself; if you like a photo, that is all that should matter. It makes little or no difference if someone else likes or dislikes it. All that matters is that *you* do, for your own personal reasons.

It is good practice to look at other photographers' pictures and use them as a guide. Be critical of those photos! Check the composition, focus, sharpness, print quality, light, dark, color balance—in short, all the basic aspects of a photograph. Remember, just because a photograph has been published, it doesn't mean that it is any good!

If you are taking photographs for yourself and don't care if they are published, then take anything you want in any fashion you please as long as it pleases you. But it is a great feeling to see your work published and to have those people who see your work respond favorably.

To get this favorable response there are some basic rules and techniques that you will need to master. Composition and positioning of the subject are greatly important to the final result. The key to success here is very simple: Think! Use your mind! Use your eyes!

Think about where in the frame that you want to place the subject; get the bits of the subject in the photograph that are important to the picture and eliminate those parts that are unnecessary or distracting.

Just because the center of the viewfinder is the focusing point, it doesn't mean that the subject should always be dead center. This is one of the most common errors, often cutting off bits of interest at the top of the frame and adding a lot of wasted space at the bottom. Use the space around the subject to work for you. When you look at a photograph (yours and others' as well), ask yourself, is it balanced? Is the composition good or bad? Is all of the subject you wanted in the photo in it? Does it have movement, a good entry or exit line, good movement to guide your eye through the picture plane? Is there depth? Do the light and dark add elements or detract? Is it better in color, or should it be black and white? Will cropping help? Lots of thoughts and questions!

Try to compose in the viewfinder, and your results will be consistently better. Most art directors, however, will say the opposite. They want room around the subject to crop the photo as they would like to see it. (Or, perhaps more accurately, how they would have taken it.) I personally try to crop in the viewfinder.

The primary element to get you started is to first decide what you want to depict, capture or accomplish before you ever pick up your camera. Then, while taking your shots, plan, analyze and check that you are on course to complete your goal. Make notes and check-lists to assure that you come back with your desired results. Composing a shot list (and even sketches of what you are looking for) can be an invaluable tool in helping you accomplish your photo goals. Before you start burning off a million frames through your camera, you must define your objectives.

## CHAPTER 2: OBJECTIVES:

What do you want to achieve? There are many aspects to a Grand Prix, dozens of stories, everything that happens from Wednesday or Thursday, when the teams are still arriving and setting up their hospitality facilities, to the mechanics, spectators, practice, qualifying, the color, race, victory, the essence of the event, weather, mood, the tearing down and departure.

The entire event is a big story and one not easily covered. Maybe just one or two aspects of it will fit your photographic needs. If you try to do the whole story, you'd better bring a lot of film, or you will just capture the obvious high points, and they aren't always the best ones.

Look for the emotion, not just with the big teams but also with the small teams—the success, the failure, the exhaustion. Don't shoot just the drivers, but get the mechanics, too. Look for that special shot or those special moments.

If you can't capture the checkered flag falling, maybe you can catch the team's response. Look past the obvious. Discover the intimate. Maybe it's just a mechanic's tool or a color or a pattern, but find something that also tells a story or sets the mood.

Maybe all you want to do is to record an image; perhaps you're out to capture the same marque of car in the same turn, in the same place, year after year after year. It's your film and your choice. Whatever you want to do, however, be sure to have objectives and plan them out. Have a shot list and check it to make sure you get what you want. Give yourself something to achieve!

When you show your photographs to your friends, it's not a time to put them to sleep. If you have the enthusiasm to show them your photos, try to make your photos explain what Formula One is. Don't just show them a photo of a car on the track; to them, that looks just like the one you just showed before and the one you're going to show next. Give them something interesting, something special to look at.

What makes a photo good? It's not only in the eye of the photographer, but also in the eye of the viewer. Give them some of the color and background, the people and the flash. They'll enjoy it a lot more, and it may excite them enough to get them interested in Formula One, too.

What about your favorite photograph? Maybe no one else likes it, but you love it. Does that make it a bad photograph? Not necessarily. Just because it's different or provocative or unusual and they don't like it, that doesn't matter. It may simply make it a question of taste. If *you* like it, that's all that should matter. First you must please yourself. I wish that I had a dollar for everyone who didn't like Picasso's work!

You must remember that you are the first one who must be pleased with your work, and if you like it, that's the most important thing. No one else has to like it—or, for that matter, even see it!

The most expensive part of going to a Grand Prix is getting there, finding a place to stay, and buying the tickets. Following that, the *cheapest* part of the whole event will probably be your film—and that will be the one thing that you will be able to enjoy for many years, jogging your memory right back to that specific race.

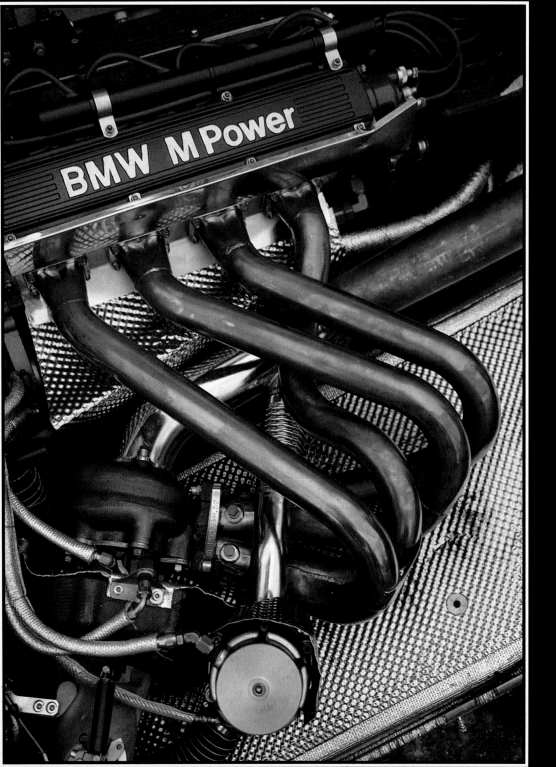

Don't be afraid to shoot film, and don't be afraid to take bad photos: we all do! It's the successful shot ratio (that is, the ratio of good photos to bad) that takes practice to get up there. The more shots you take the better you will get, and the more photos you will find that are really good. Practice is your best ally in photography; the more you shoot, the better you get.

Your primary objective should be to concentrate. Think about your photographs; don't just point and shoot. Give some thought to what you want to accomplish photographically during your racing weekend. Think about what you want to achieve and head in that direction. But keep your eyes open for that extra-special shot or moment.

Decide early whether you want to capture the whole event, the essence of the race, or just a special part of it. Plan your shots and your race; your photographs will be better off for it. Think about what you want to capture: the practice, the race, the spectators, the teams, the officials, the drivers, the background, color, details, cars, atmosphere, mood, action, portraits, weather, the essence of the event, the complete story or just one special objective. . . it's your choice. Give it some thought beforehand and your results will be dramatically better.

There is so much to see and so many photos to shoot that sometimes you become overwhelmed if you just show up and start shooting at everything that moves. Plan and think; make your shot list and plan what you want to accomplish. Check your list periodically to make sure that everything you came to do is being accomplished. It is easy to become distracted as there is so much going on. Learn to focus your attention on your objectives, but don't become so tunnel-visioned that you don't see the special and unique things happening around you, too.

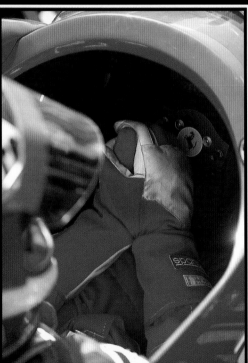

## CHAPTER 3: PLANNING

The most important aspect of planning is getting to know the circuit. Get to know where the best photographs are, and when you should shoot them. I try to walk the entire circuit before the racing weekend starts; it is especially important to walk the entire circuit of a Grand Prix that is new, or one that I haven't been to in quite some time, or one that may have undergone many modifications. Walk the circuit the opposite direction the cars run; if you walk the same direction they run, you will see what the *driver* sees, not what your camera will see.

Try to walk at the same time of day that you will be photographing so you can see where the light falls on the scene and cars. You will see what choice of location you have to photograph from. Can you get to your chosen site? Can you get away from it after your shooting, or will you be stuck there for all the session? You will be able to see where the light is coming and going at what time of the day.

One of the first things to notice is where the light source is. It is very important to remember where the light is at what time of the day and what direction it is coming from and what direction it is going. If it is a bright and sunny day, the light should be behind you for the best exposures. The general rule is that if you can see your shadow to the front of you, the exposure on the car or person should be at its best, unless you consciously choose a dramatic side-lit or back-lit subject.

To get the best shots you must get to know the circuit and find out exactly where your pass or ticket will allow you to go. Don't forget, some of the best overviews of any race are from the grandstand. When choosing your location, walk the entire circuit, if possible, and find the best site your ticket or photo pass allows you to use.

The best procedure for walking the circuit is to walk the direction the cars will be coming from; that is to say, study the circuit against the direction of traffic. You'll want to look for rear shots, too, but most shots will be head on, three-quarter front, or full-profile pan shots, so you will want to see what the background and locations will be like. Find your location and wait for the cars to come.

Actually walking on the circuit might not be possible after the Wednesday or Thursday before the race; besides, it's better to concentrate on the same area that you will be photographing from, so you'll know what lens to use from that spot.

Just a sidebar of importance here: *Never* cross the circuit when it is *technically hot*. All photographers in Formula One must be off the circuit and behind the barriers half an hour before the track goes hot. *Never* cross the circuit or cross the barriers during a black- or red-flag situation; the circuit is still considered *hot*. Be sure that you can get to that favorite spot *safely and legally* as well as getting away from there, too; many a photographer has been stuck in a spot for a whole session or removed once the session came alive because the location was deemed unsafe or a "Zone Rouge." Remember, *think*, use good sense, and plan ahead. If you want to move around during the race, plan your movements from location to location, and find out where the "red zones" are before getting stuck in one.

If possible, have tickets for more than one location to provide you with more mobility and access. If you don't have the luxury of a press pass and the circuit has the option for "Super-Photo-Pass" or Paddock Club tickets, these will allow you much better access than just a grandstand seat—but they are expensive.

At some circuits there are special photo towers just for spectators with Canon cameras. On these towers you can use your own camera body on a full range of telephoto lenses available at the tower.

Plan each pre-race day as well as your weekend so that you are able to cover all of your objectives. Determine how much film you have to use in each location and with each subject, and carry enough so you don't run out, but don't carry too much if it is a hot or rainy day. Heat will damage your film, and if rain gets in the film cannister, it's all but history! Be sure, though, to have a little bit of extra film, just in case you have that opportunity for that extra-special shot you hadn't expected. Of course, if you do have extra film, have it ready and loaded in your camera; it won't do you any good in your camera bag! Remember, racing is full of the unexpected—so plan for it!

Preparation is a very important part of photography. You must plan not only your equipment (that is, what to use, where to use it, where the sun is, and so on), but also where the action or that special shot is going to be. Usually, the best place to be is at the entrance or the exit of a turn or a series of turns. Knowing the circuit is mandatory in determining where to be and when to be there. Instinct has a lot to do with it, but so does planning—and so does chance.

On the straightaway the cars are all going tremendously fast, and there is little of interest except a spectacular background and a blur of color; for best results try working in the corners. The better you know your sport and all aspects of it, the better photographs you will take.

For those of you who are really serious about motor racing photography, try to take a high performance driving course. Get into the car and learn to drive at the limit (it doesn't necessarily have to be at the *car's* limit, just yours). Learn what a driver must do so that you will better understand what the car will be doing at any given moment on the race track.

The better you know what a car is going to do from the driver's seat, the better you will know what a car is going to do when it's coming at you on the circuit while you are trying to photograph it. There are many good driving schools; two I prefer in the U.S. are the Bob Bondurant School of High Performance Driving and the Bertil Roos School. There are other good schools, too, and really any school is better than none, but these two will give you a good understanding of what motor racing is all about, as well as make you a lot better street driver.

## CHAPTER 4:   FILM AND EXPOSURE

What kind of film? Color transparency (slide) film! Why? It forces you to become a better photographer faster, and it is actually cheaper to shoot that print film. It has less latitude in exposure, so you have to get the exposure right;  usually the  best exposure range is about 1/4 stop over or 1/2 stop underexposed, maximum. If you have a choice of film, then my recommendation is easy:  Kodachrome!

 I find 64 ISO the best all-around film speed.  The quality, the color fidelity, the sharpness, the contrast, the grain structure, and the overall consistency are of an extremely high standard. If you are doing scenic or still shots, Kodachrome 25 ISO has even better grain and color characteristics. There is now even a Kodachrome 200 ISO for that little extra speed on dark days, but my preference is still  64 ISO.

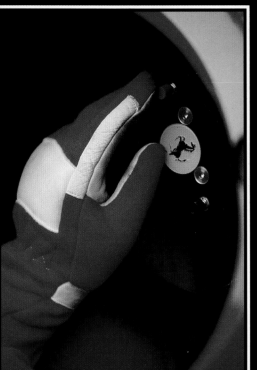

Why Kodachrome? The archival characteristics of the film are the best on the market. Kodachrome has a tremendous life span, and when properly stored it has little or no fading or color shifting after it is processed. If projected frequently, however, it, too, will fade, although not as fast as other transparency films. Kodachrome is as archival as you can get (at least for now).

The negative aspect of Kodachrome is that it must be processed by Kodak or a major processing company that has the Kodak rights and equipment to do it, which can take anywhere from overnight to one week for results, depending on how close you are to a Kodachrome processing facility.

Some countries don't have Kodachrome processing at all, while others have same-day service. Personally, of those that I have used, I prefer the processing in the US, Germany, and Australia to all the others that I have used because of their quick turnaround and generally scratch-free results.

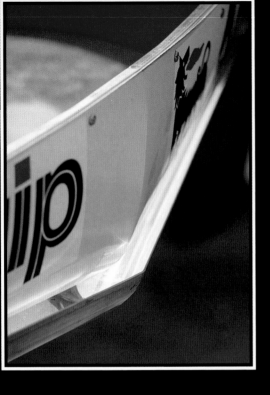

If you need results quickly, one hour to overnight, I recommend Fujichrome 50 ISO or 100 ISO and Ektachrome 100 ISO. (Remember, as a rule, the lower the ISO the finer the grain and the sharper your results.) You can buy faster film, 200 ISO and 400 ISO, but the grain and sharpness are not quite as good as the slower ISO film, and unless it is really dark you must use either a very high shutter speed or a very small aperture, or both.

With Fujichrome and Ektachrome, the archival qualities of the film construction are traded for a quick developing process that most processing facilities can handle. You can even process it yourself with a Unicolor developing set and chemicals. Be careful, though, as poor water quality and the wrong temperature can greatly affect the quality of the results.

Color print film has a lot better exposure latitude, but is not as good for press-printed reproduction, and with age its archival qualities are questionable. Standard color prints from negatives fade at a quite rapid rate if placed in the sun or exposed to a lot of daylight, and they simply fade or change color due to age.

If you are interested in color prints to display, I recommend Kodachrome film; have your best pictures printed on Ilford Cibachrome paper at a custom printing lab. You must specify Cibachrome or you might get a standard "R-Type" paper print, which is nice, too, but not in the same league, and it is not archival. Cibachrome is not only beautiful, with fully saturated color that is extremely sharp, but it's the closest thing on the market to archival film.

By the way, if you want prints from slides but you don't want the expense of Cibachrome, get "R-type" prints. Avoid the extra step and cost of an internegative (unless you are looking for a mural-sized print) that some photo shops will try to talk you into; the fewer generations it takes from original to print, the better the final print quality will be, and on "R-type" paper the print is made directly from the transparency. An "R-type" print might cost a few cents more and might take a day or so longer to make, but the quality will definitely be better.

Many people still regard black-and-white as the only true photographic art, partly because of its archival qualities if it is done properly and partly for the mood and tonal ranges combined with the contrast of light and dark. This is an opinion that is finally being altered, due in part to Kodachrome and now the Cibachrome print process.

Early color prints were done by an expensive and time-consuming dye transfer process that is now giving way to the Cibachrome process. Black-and-white still has many followers, but if you don't process and print yourself, the higher cost and the difficulty in getting good quality has made it far less attractive than color negatives and the "one-hour processing" shops. But a good black-and-white print is still an art form in itself.

Many publications will accept only black-and-white prints, and others, due to their deadlines, require the submission of raw, undeveloped film. The most consistent black-and-white film on the market, and one that has been the choice of professionals for years, is Kodak Tri-X Pan. If developed properly, the grain characteristics and sharpness are excellent, but the speed is a bit fast at 400 ISO. But high-speed film can be a deterrent to the creative process; under most conditions it forces you to use higher shutter speeds and get more depth-of-field than you might want.

Ilford HP5 is an excellent film, too and has characteristics and speed very similar to Tri-X. Panatomic X by Kodak is exceptional for large prints, as the grain is extremely fine and the sharpness good, but it is a bit slow for motor racing. (It's great for nudes, though!)

If you want an ultra-high-speed film that is very sharp and has a full grey range, try Kodak 2475 recording film. It has a lot of grain, but it is really sharp. (Grain and sharpness are sometimes confused; they are different items. A film can be fine-grained and not sharp or it can be coarse-grained and ultra-sharp; it depends on the design of the particular film and how it is developed.)

2475 is great for night shooting, like at Daytona or Le Mans. I don't use flash with this film and I normally expose it at about 1200 ISO, but I have pushed it to 12,000 ISO and higher and it still provided me an image I could use!

Black-and-white is beautiful and dramatic. It creates a wonderful mood when done correctly; and of course it is essential for tight deadline work.

If price is a major consideration in deciding what film you will use, then Kodachrome with Kodak-authorized processing is the best value for money; the only prints you need to make are those which you really like. Even if you can't afford Cibachrome prints, Kodak and their licensed agents do an excellent job with their "R-type" prints; if you don't like the way they turn out, have them do it again! It won't cost you any more. You can even get poster-sized prints from them at a great price; but remember, they will fade with age and sunlight.

If you are doing black-and-white, try processing it and printing it yourself; you'll save a lot of money and probably get better quality, plus it can be a lot of fun.

You might want to consider bulk-loading your film. Bulk film usually comes in 100-foot or thirty-meter rolls and is available in most black-and-white films as well as Fujichrome and Ektachrome, but Kodachrome is not available in bulk. Ilford film cassettes are re-usable, while Kodak's are not. The film cassettes you buy especially for bulk loading are a bit expensive, but they are re-useable. Be sure, however, if someone else processes your bulk-loaded film, that they save the cannisters and return them to you.

By the way, in the mail or during other forms of shipping, often the re-loaded cannisters pop open and the film is usually fogged. If a cannister does come open, process the film anyway, after quickly getting it back in the cannister. Usually you still can save some of the shots near the center of the roll. With this in mind, if you are sending raw film somewhere for deadline publication, you might be safer by sending factory-loaded film. Your art director will be much happier, too.

But if you are on a tight budget or you do your processing yourself, then bulk-loading usually saves about 50%, and it's easy; all you need is a light-tight film-changing bag, a daylight bulk loader, a roll of bulk film, some film cassettes, scissors, and artist's tape to tape the film end to the cassette.

Be careful of your film; don't subject it to extremes of temperature. Care of your film before, during, and after exposure is extremely important to get and maintain the best results. Keep your film fresh and in a cool place. Buy just what you are going to need and make sure the photo store where you buy it has fresh film stored in a cool place. Usually a store which has high-volume film sales will have the freshest film; you probably won't have any problem if you deal with a photo store that caters to the professional.

If you have to purchase a large quantity, refrigerate it. *Don't freeze it; just keep it cool.* Keep it out of all heat you possibly can. If you refrigerate, don't forget to give the cool film sufficient time to stabilize to the temperature and conditions you are shooting in. If used too soon after refrigeration, there can be a great difference in atmospheric temperature. This can cause condensation on the film which will also get on the inside of your camera and can ruin a whole roll of shots. If the film is too cold, the speed might alter, giving the film effectively less speed (ISO) than it says on the film cannister. This goes for extremely cold weather, too. Kodachrome's ISO seems to be the least affected by cold. Lots to think about and remember, but your results will also be a lot better!

Now for something simple: What's the best film for the beginner—or for the expert? I feel that the best film, not only to learn with but to continue with after you have perfected your technique, is Kodachrome 64.

If you are unable to find it in your location then you might try Fujichrome 100. Both films will teach you you to refine your photographic technique and get the best color, sharpness and grain quality presently available.

But they are not that forgiving and you don't have much latitude. You will overexpose and underexpose and have a bit of trouble getting the exposures right at first, but at least this process will quickly tell you whether your camera's meter exposes correctly! It will teach you how to get a good exposure,too: Half a stop overexposed and the photo will be washed out; half a stop under, and it will be too dark!

You can't save an overexposed slide, short of duping it onto black-and-white film and printing it as a black-and-white print; the color will wash out too much. Underexposed film is a bit different; it can be lightened by duping, but it is costly and time-consuming. The best thing to do is expose it properly in the first place. ·

With Kodachrome you can't alter the processing time unless you want to pay a small fortune; all you can do is expose it right the first time to get the desired results. (Some authorized Kodak labs do have the ability to push-process Kodachrome, but it is expensive and not readily available). At first it may be disappointing to see poorly-exposed transparencies; with prints, you have a lot of latitude, and even the poorly-exposed photos usually will have an image, even if the color isn't perfect. But that won't teach you to expose properly.

You must consider whether you want just an image, an archival record, or simply a good photograph. If you want a good photograph, then you must realize that not every picture that you take will be a prize-winner; it takes a lot of work and thought to create good photographs. It is not just simply a matter of pushing the button and presto, a great photo—no matter what the commercials tell you!

With some of the automatic cameras, the "presto" image has been created by the company's marketing department. Automatic cameras are great, but not perfect, and they won't teach you to be Henri Cartier-Bresson. Automatic cameras create an image, usually in acceptable or near-correct exposure. Some of them even do the focusing for you! But, alas, they all lack the human aspect of creativity and free thought. That is where you come in. You can over-ride their automatic ability and exercise your creativity far beyond their limitations. You must make the camera do what you need, not let the camera dictate the terms of your photography.

If you use Kodachrome 64, here is a basic guide to start you out with a point of reference. In full sun (no overcast) with the sun at your back, your exposure should probably be 1/250 of a second between f8 and f11. I say *probably* because 1/500 *can* be used between f5.6 and f8, but you decrease your depth of field and you tend to stop the wheels too much, thus decreasing the feeling of motion and speed. With a long lens, however (500mm or 600mm), you will want to use 1/500 to eliminate camera movement, and probably a monopod as well.

An exposure of 1/250 works well for head-on shots, fast pan shots, or general scenic shots. If you are getting camera movement or your photos aren't sharp at 1/250, then try 1/500 and practice until it is easy to get good results at that speed before going back to the slower shutter speeds again. You will still get some wheel and background movement, but not as much. Practice; see what works best for you. A lot of professionals don't even consider using 1/250, believing it too slow—but their static backgrounds and frozen wheels show it.

If you are shooting into the sun or with your subject backlit (this is generally for portraits only), set your exposure to f5.6 at 1/250 of a second. (If your car on the track is backlit, then you will have an overexposed shot at this exposure; if the car on the track is backlit, you are better off to use your normal exposure and make the car darker and more dramatic, or open just 1/2 stop to f8 and take in more light. You will generally be better off to try to avoid backlit shots, except for dramatic effect, because you tend to get a lot of glare and highlight flare. You can get rid of the glare if you use a polarizing filter, but you will also greatly reduce the light entering the camera.)

Experiment and practice! Remember, you're the one you have to please, so get the results that you like best. These exposure guides are not carved in stone; they are simply a starting point. 1/250 might just be too slow a shutter speed for you to get consistently good results. Again, practice and see what works best for you.

## CHAPTER 5: EQUIPMENT

To start out, the best all-around, easiest camera for photographing race cars is a hand-held 35mm single-lens-reflex camera. The most important thing is to develop good technique and skills; this can be done with any SLR, it doesn't have to be new and expensive. Old, used, and cheaper cameras won't make you any less creative than a brand-new expensive SLR system.

Develop good photographic technique first, then worry about getting a better camera! If you can't take a good photo with an old or mechanical camera, then chances are you won't take a good one with a new and expensive one, either; in fact, it might be even worse! But if you can take good photos with not-so-good cameras, then you will probably improve with more sophisticated equipment. More important is the lens, not simply the camera body. Your lenses must be of good quality. That's really what is important!

What equipment should you have? Well, don't just rush out and buy a ton of camera gear. Give it some thought, even if you have the money and can afford whatever you want. As far as what *kind* of camera to buy, there are a couple of things to look for. First and most important (after a good range of inter-changeable lenses that will fit it), make sure that you can have *shutter priority*. For motor racing this is extremely important. That means that you can set the speed of the shutter, not just hope that the camera will set the shutter-speed fast enough or slow enough to get the results that you want. You need to be able to control the shutter speed and choose 1/125, 1/250, or 1/500 of a second or whatever speed you want, when you want it, not when the camera tells you to. Some cameras even give you the option for speeds in between, such as 1/90, 1/180, and 1/350 of a second; these are even better, as you have more control over your expo-sure.

Now that you've chosen a camera body, what lens or lenses should you buy? You might try renting some different ones before buying one; that way you can see what works best for you. You must be comfortable with your equipment or you won't have good results, no matter what it costs.

I prefer lenses that are manufactured by the cam-era maker to ones that are after market accessories. This is a personal preference. The cost is also much higher, but I find the quality to be more consistent.

I prefer a lens of a fixed focal length to one of a zoom variety, although the current quality of zoom lenses is almost as good. But probably the best starting kit for the novice photographer is a mid-range zoom lens (80-200mm) and a wide-angle of about 20 to 24mm. For me, you can't get a wide-angle lens too wide; I like the distortion it creates. If you decide to get a 300mm telephoto, then I would recommend a 135mm to fill in for portraits and the middle range.

For many years I worked with just a 300mm, a 135mm, and a 20mm on an ancient Nikon ratchet-advancing camera body without a motor drive. It was difficult, but I managed. (I had a 50mm, too, but didn't use it much. Still don't.)

If you have the opportunity to work in the pits, zoom lenses are really handy, but extreme wide-angles and telephotos are interesting, too. The telephoto lenses (300 to 500mm) give a very dramatic feeling to the photograph; they compress and accentuate the heat vapors if it is very warm. They will also blow out the background to shapeless colors and patterns if used at close range, perhaps for a detail shot or portrait.

The wide-angle lens will fill the frame but distort and bend certain elements of the photograph. With a 15 or 20mm lens you can work very close to the car and driver and get some really creative angles that will increase the distortion and get the whole thing in the photo. A 7.5mm fish-eye can be a lot of fun, too.

But working with a wide angle lens can be dangerous; if a car is approaching in the pits and you are looking through the lens as it comes up to you, it really is a lot closer than it appears; in fact, if it fills the frame, it probably just hit you! Be careful. Know your equipment and know your sport. The better you know them the better work you will do and the safer you'll be.

Speaking of safety, think of your cameras, too. You must protect your equipment as much as possible, but not at the expense of missing a great shot. Avoid the obvious problems: Don't drop camera or lens, don't touch the shutter inside the camera, keep the lens clean, clean the camera and lenses well after extremely wet or dusty working conditions. With this in mind it is probably a good idea to invest in a filter and keep it on the lens all of the time to protect it. I'd recommend a skylight filter, which doesn't cut down on the amount of light entering the lens, but cuts down on haze. Working without a filter can cause a few expensive hazards, like stone chips on the front lens element. Improper or excessive cleaning can wear through the lens coating, causing color modification and loss of sharpness.

best. The top-of-the-line models also have an ability to read flash, too.

Incident-light meters are used with the sphere (white ball) facing the camera lens. This sphere has to be in the same light as the subject (sometimes a problem) and facing right at the camera lens. The head of the meter swivels so the reading can be taken, and the digital ones will hold the exposure in memory till you get back to the camera position. For best results read the instructions of the one that you buy!

If you have the notion to get a long lens (that is, one over 300mm), then you should really get a monopod to steady both camera and lens. A tripod tends to make the work a bit too tight and controlled, but a monopod will allow freedom of motion and will work with your body movements. Getz makes an excellent one.

There is a place for tripods, too, but I feel that they are bulky, hard to move, and get in the way of not only you but your working companions. Also, they restrict positive camera movement (that is, easy, fluid and creative movement) and they tend to stifle the spontaneous creative process. Other than that, they are delightful things to lug around up and down a three-mile circuit. The last time I used one was with a 4x5 view camera—and I don't miss either one!

But if you're using a lens of over 600mm with shutter speeds under 1/500 of a second, I would definitely recommend a tripod. Again, Getz is one of the best on the market. They are not cheap—but don't cut corners on equipment that you are going to keep for a long time. Cheap stuff will fall apart; a Getz will last a lifetime. I have a thirty-year-old Majestic tripod that is just as good—and just as heavy!—as the day I bought it, and it still does its job perfectly.

As you become more proficient and more serious, is strongly recommend that you use two cameras with different lenses to save time changing foca lengths—and also to provide a backup if you have failure with one. You will usually do better to stick with one brand and build a system in that direction so you have more versatility and interchangeabil ity.

Also, different makes of cameras focus in differen directions. That is, you turn the lens-focusing ring in a clockwise or anti-clockwise direction—so i you decide you need two different camera systems it is better to get two that focus in the same direc tion. If not, it takes a great deal of shooting to become accustomed to focusing differently for each camera. It can be done, but it does slow you down until you get used to it, and you always seem to find yourself trying to focus in the wrong direction when you're in a hurry.

The better you know your camera system, the more you get better and faster at getting a good shot. Pick a camera system that you can grow into, not grow out of, as your technique improves. You want a camera system that will eventually wear out, not be outgrown. Give it a lot of thought and research: the camera system you choose must be easy for you to use and comfortable to handle; it must fit you hand, have a good viewing system for *you*, and give you good long-term wear. Start with the basic ele ments of a system that you can expand as you needs grow and change.

Now that you've planned what you want to accomplish, will your camera system allow you to do it? Your best bet for overall good results is the basic 35mm single-lens-reflex system. When choosing equipment, find a system that is versatile and that will not be outdated rapidly. Camera technology is rapidly changing, and you are better off to stay with one of the primary manufacturers.

The addition of motor drives; telephoto, wide-angle, and zoom lenses; and various accessories is dependent on your level of knowledge and your need to achieve specific results. Learn what your camera system will do with every addition. Then add something else *after* you've mastered what you just added. Don't add a lot of new bits at once, or you might be overwhelmed by the equipment, concentrating on the hardware instead of your original photographic objectives.

Get to know the equipment that you have and feel comfortable with it before you start getting more expensive, exotic bits and pieces. You must learn to drive before you learn to race!

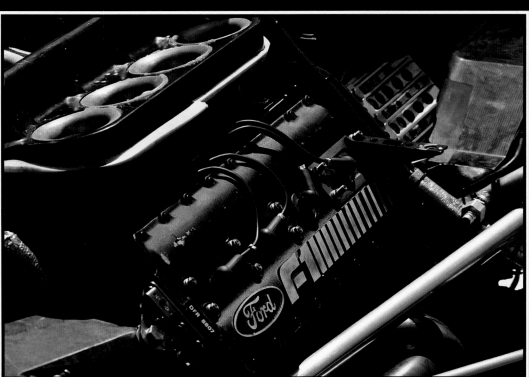

Most of the major camera manufacturers have a full range of professional lenses and camera bodies that are fully interchangeable with most of their beginning equipment. I recommend, when you purchase a camera system, that you invest in a system that can be built on, one that you won't outgrow. Get one that you can add to as you become more sophisticated.

It's a good idea to carry an extra rangefinder auto-focus camera with built-in motor and flash; they're great for quick shooting in the pits, at parties, or wherever something special might be happening. They usually come with a small case to put them right on your belt. Many come with zoom lenses to give even greater flexibility; they're quick and accurate, give you good exposures, and stay out of the way unless you need them. (Which, come to think of it, might also describe the ideal photographic assistant!)

Rangefinder autofocus cameras are unobtrusive when taking candid shots. They may look amateur-ish, but you can get professional results. There are a lot of them on the market now, some with tele-photo lenses, some with zooms. Look and study them; they are meant to be an additional camera, not a primary one, so keep that in mind if you get one and make sure that it has infra-red focusing, or you might have trouble in the dark.

For motorsports and action photography in general, shutter priority is essential on any automatic system mode. Make sure that your camera's metering system is both versatile and accurate. When buying, try to get a camera that has spot, center-weighted, and full-frame light averaging. The meter system must read most colors correctly, which is not the case with many camera systems. Try them out before buying. Rent them if you have to, but make sure they do what you want them to do before you buy.

Metering accuracy in adverse conditions is essential. But by using the exposure system that I have explained earlier, you will have a formula to get a proper exposure in full sunlit conditions without any meter at all. It also allows you to compare your meter's reading to the known formula to determine whether your meter is reading correctly. The exposure system is a constant, thereby giving the same exposure quality anywhere you are, with any kind of film, as long as the sun is full and at your back.

Just a quick refresher: Let's start with a constant of 1/250 for the shutter speed so the only change you will have is the f-stop for films of different speeds, indicated by ISO numbers. (Those f-stop numbers refer to the size of the aperture, but don't worry about the actual significance of the numbers. Just remember that the larger the f-stop, the smaller the aperture, and the less light coming in for any given amount of time. Hence f22 is a very *small* aperture, while f1.8 and f2 are comparatively huge.)

With these film speeds, use these f-stops in bright sunlight:

64 ISO, between f8 and f11
100 ISO, f11
200 ISO, f16
400 ISO, f22.

Remember, if you increase or decrease your shutter speed, you must also increase or decrease the amount of light entering the lens by opening or closing the aperture. For example, using 100 ISO film with a 1/500 shutter speed, you would have an f-stop (aperture) of f8; at 1/1000 it would be f5.6. But at 1/125 it would be f16, and f22 at 1/60. Don't forget, this only works in bright sun coming from behind you; you must be able to see your shadow!

# CHAPTER 6:  COMPOSITION

When I started writing this book I promised that I wouldn't waste a lot of time and space on composition. (After all, there are thousands of art and photographic books for sale just about composition and design, inter-relating elements contrasting this and that, most of them so boring that you'd fall off your chair trying to forge through them. But it has to be in here, so let's get to it.) Perhaps it is the best idea for the serious photographer to read as many varied books on photography as possible. On art, too; in art classes as well as art books you will really learn the basics of balance and good compostion.

When composing photographs, the most common error made by the novice photographer (and many short-sighted professionals, too) is directly related to the equipment. Modern camera designers have decided that every photograph should have the center of attention in the center of the viewfinder. Wrong! That's usually the only place it *shouldn't* be; but that's precisely where they put the *focusing grid.*

Ok, so you have to focus with it; but then move the camera so the subject is in a more interesting place in the viewfinder. Top? Bottom? Side? Who knows? It depends on the photo—and the vision of the photographer. It's your eye and your photo, so make it interesting.

One common photojournalistic practice is the *rule of thirds*. Draw two imaginary horizontal lines across your composition, dividing it into thirds. Add two vertical lines, again dividing it into thirds, and you will now have four intersecting lines. The *intersections* of these lines are generally the points of most interest in a well-composed photograph. I say *generally*, as it really depends on the subject, color and other balance in the photo, but it is a good place to start. But don't stop there, experiment!

Don't get trapped into shooting just horizontal shots just because that's the way the camera is designed; vertical images are exciting and dynamic. (Verticals are perfect for portraits.) A diagonal image is interesting, too, especially in a pan shot; run that car from one corner to the other, right across the diagonal of the frame. Place the subject in the proper spot in the first place and you won't have to crop it later; learn to "crop it in the viewfinder." This is the best place to do it (although there are thousands of art directors who will disagree!). Take the time to *compose* your photo; don't just point and snap, point and snap. Look, see, and control your image.

If you have the opportunity, get into the paddock, or join a pit walk-about. Think of the various bits and pieces lying around as "still life." The various mechanical pieces, the motor, the injectors, the exhausts: They don't move around a lot, so you can take your time to compose in the viewfinder.

One word of caution: If you are lucky enough to be in the pit or paddock area, you are the intruder, so stay out of the way of the mechanics. They have a job to do, and they don't appreciate people—anybody!—in their way or moving or touching the car parts; so look (and shoot), but don't touch. If there is something that you'd really like to photograph and you just can't get close enough without being in the way, ask the team manager if it's all right to get closer; if it isn't, he'll tell you. If he says it's okay, so much the better and you'll get your shot.

The range of color is another element of composition, just as the shades of grey that make up light and dark. With a still life or with an action shot, all these elements make up the balance of the photograph. Some photographs are most outstanding because of their simplicity; others work because of their complexity.

Grand Prix is probably the most colorful of sports, always varied and always changing. Look for the juxtaposition of colors, some balancing the others, some at odds. Look again. Look at the colors creating lines leading into the photo, those coming out. Look at the movement within the viewfinder. Look at the background. What is in the photo that is not the primary subject?

Beware of the background; does the driver have a telephone pole coming out of his head? In a recent motor-racing magazine of international distribution, there were two top drivers, posing with their car for a formal portrait—and someone in the background was mooning the cameras! No one noticed during the shoot, and the art director (naturally!) missed it during layout and paste-up; the photo was already on the news-stands before anyone saw it.

Look at what you're seeing! See what is going on in the entire scene—or someday you, too, might be surprised at what's in your photo!

Photographers, like the teachers of defensive driving courses, sometimes talk about getting the big picture. Often the horizon will establish the firmest baseline of your photograph; is the horizon line straight, or does it look like it was shot from a boat in heavy seas? As a matter of fact, where *is* the horizon line? If it's dead center, move it somewhere else—anyplace *but* dead center. Look where your subject is; do you need more room in front, in the rear, on the top, or at the bottom? What lens are you using, and how does it affect your subject? An ultra-wide-angle will wrap the subject right around you; an extreme telephoto will compress it and bring it close. It all depends on what you want, what you visualize, and how you regard your subject.

*Look! See! Visualize!*

## CHAPTER 7: CAMERA TECHNIQUE

The elimination of variables in photography gives you the opportunity to create. If you haven't eliminated the variables, you will be thinking about them and not fully seeing your subject. Try to establish as many constants in your photographic technique as possible, and you will have more time to think creatively, because you'll need less time to think about the mechanical aspects of taking a photo.

The most important factor in consistently taking good photographs, regardless of the subject matter or what kind of camera you own, is simple: *Practice! Practice! Practice!* The actual implementation of technique requires a lot of practice and is oftentimes disappointing, but when you get it right it's worth the time, money, and film it took trying to get it. Much of the development of an individual technique is really experimentation, taking creative chances and trying to make new concepts work.

The easiest subjects to photograph are still or static. Here your subject doesn't move around and you have plenty of time to consider all the principles of shape, linear movement, light and dark and color to achieve the desired result. You even have time to try a variety of different shots.

The better you know your camera, the better your results will be. The same can be said for your film; learn what it will do and what it won't do. At what shutter speed can you effectively hand-hold your telephoto lens? Will a half-stop under exposure work in a given situation? You will generally not want to use shutter speeds slower than 1/250 except in very low light or for special effects, nor faster than 1/500 unless you are trying to freeze all motion.

When using slower speeds, you can usually hand-hold a normal lens down to about 1/30 of a second, but if you are shooting any slower you're better off using a monopod, a tripod, or some other brace so you don't get camera movement when you press the shutter. Since a telephoto greatly aggravates camera movement, usually 1/125 of a second is the slowest speed for a hand-held camera with a telephoto, although I have shot at 1/30 with my 300mm in very poor light conditions. You just have to hold your breath and squeeze the shutter ever so softly—a little prayer can't hurt!—but you can do it if you are careful.

A good general rule when setting shutter speeds is to use a shutter speed about equal to the effective focal length of the lens. In other words, for an 800mm lens use 1/1000 of a second, for a 500mm lens use 1/500, use 1/250 for a 300mm or a 200mm. With this basic guide you shouldn't get camera movement, but that depends on how gently you press the shutter and how you hold your camera. Remember to squeeze the shutter gently. (A soft shutter release is available for most manual cameras and the new ones with motor drives are usually very sensitive to the touch, so you don't have to worry too much.)

While shooting a moving subject with any camera-lens combination, steadiness is vital. Take a solid stance with feet firmly planted in a line directly under your shoulders. Keep your arms and elbows in close to your body, brace the bottom of the camera and/or the lens with your focusing hand. Your other hand should be free to trigger the shutter release and advance the film, unless your camera has a self-winder or motor-drive.

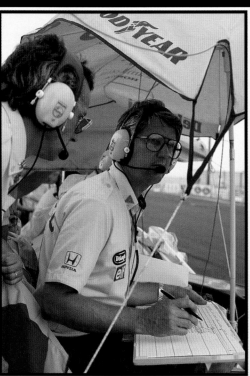

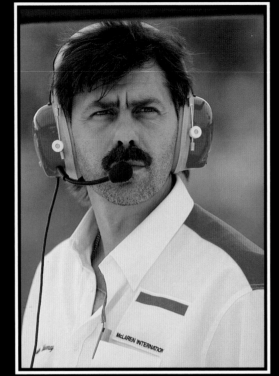

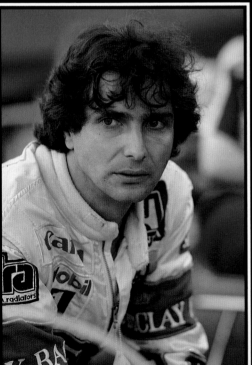

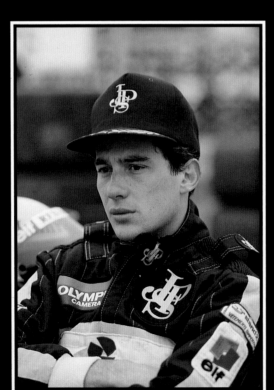

Should you believe your meter or not? Is it accurate? Is it "color blind?" You have to have a basis for comparison. If you are not sure, here is one way of simplifying the exposure process and eliminating another variable. Get to know one type of film and its characteristics. As explained before, using Kodak Kodachrome 64 ISO in bright sun, with the sun at your back (you can see your shadow), you will generally want an exposure of 1/250 of a second between f8 and f11 (f9.3). If you *facing* the sun, on the other hand, say for a portrait with the subject's back to sun, you have to increase your exposure by about 1-1/2 stops, so shoot at 1/250 at about f5.6.

For back-lit portraits, it is often good to consider using a fill flash to balance the exposure to the background. This is really easy with auto-focus cameras; just turn the flash on. With more sophisticated cameras, it will require some testing to see what works best with your camera and flash combination. In any test, be sure to document your test accurately so you know which exposure created which results.

Don't just rely on flash for your portraits; try to use natural light wherever possible. Flash can be very irritating to the drivers, who are bombarded by flash at every race. The essence of good photography is waiting for the right shot; so wait with a telephoto. Forget the flash and the photo will be definitely more intimate.

Your motor racing shots should have more to them than just a car on a track. Try to get more than one car in the photo, or a whole grouping. There should be more to your photograph than just some racing cars on some anonymous track; there should be mood, feeling, and movement. The frozen shot is usually sharp, clear—and boring. It might just as well have been achieved by parking the car in the desired position on the track, without any risk or excitement.

If your photographs are all taken at a thousandth of a second (many times even a five-hundredth), they will show wheels that are frozen, cars that seem to be parked, and an unblurred background, producing a generally static feeling. Better to shoot at 1/250 and pan with the motion of the car, giving your photo movement, life, and a feeling of speed.

Remember that the depth of field (the sharp area of the photograph that is in acceptable focus) decreases in proportion to the speed of the shutter; the higher the shutter speed, the more shallow the depth of field. The aperture also affects the depth of field; the larger the aperture, the narrower your depth of field. Finally, longer lenses also decrease your depth of field, so if you are using telephoto lenses at high speed with large apertures, you have to focus very carefully indeed!

For subjects moving at the speed of modern racing cars, it is vitally important to pre-focus on a given spot and wait for the car to reach the focus point before depressing the shutter. If you try to follow focus—actually changing your focus with the moving subject—you usually can't do it fast enough, and you'll be very disappointed with the results, as most of your photos will be out of focus. In one's earliest attempts at learning to follow-focus, one tends to over-focus, then under-focus, much like a novice driver correcting a sliding car; it may fishtail all over the road before coming back under control. The difference is that the car you are trying to take a photo of has now gone out of the picture, and you have nothing left to focus on!

The best procedure is to pick a spot in the frame that you want the car to fill, focus on that point, check it with a couple of cars passing through the focus zone, and then wait for your shot. As the car approaches, follow it with the camera until it reaches the focus zone, then gently press the shutter. There is no need to take a motor drive sequence, as there is only one point at which the focus will be perfect (unless you have an ultra-high-speed motor-drive taking 8-10 frames per second, catching your subject several times before it leaves your zone of focus).

For a start-of-the-race shot, however, you will want your motor-drive cranking out photos at high speed as the cars come through your focus point. Don't try to change focus, just let them drive through your focus point as you shoot. With practice—and luck—your focus point will be where the action is!

Try this exercise: With the car coming straight at you (or easier yet, with the car stopped) at a distance of a hundred feet or so, shoot with Kodachrome 64 ISO with your camera set at f8-f11 at 1/250; this should give the entire car a sharp focus, from nose to rear wing. Then shoot again at f5.6-f8 at a five hundredth; this will reduce the sharp area (the depth of field) to an area starting just in front of the windscreen and ending somewhere toward the rear of the engine cover.

Nor is this depth of field evenly distributed; the area of sharpness runs one third in front of your ideal focus point and two thirds behind it. Thus at f8-f11, you should focus on a point near the car's steering wheel. Unfortunately, you can't quite see the wheel, so you have to anticipate where it is and practice a lot to get your hand-eye coordination going to focus where it ought to be.

If you think it's difficult to get most of the car in acceptable focus, think about the difficulties involved in the *pan shot*, moving the camera with the car to create the illusion of speed. One the most difficult techniques to master, panning involves moving the camera parallel to the moving subject at the same relative speed during the exposure to blur the background while keeping the subject in sharp focus. The technique is simple, but requires a lot of practice. Choose a shutter speed of 1/60 for slow-moving subjects, 1/125 for medium speed in turns, and 1/250 for high-speed panning. For ultra-high-speed cars moving at 150 to 200mph plus, you have to pan at a five hundredth or you will still get vertical movement.

To position yourself ideally, pick a hypothetical point within the radius of the turn so that the car will be moving through the turn at a constant radius to your position. Assume a stance that will place your feet directly beneath your shoulders, face the position where the exposure is to be made, pre-focus on the desired spot where the car will pass through the focus plane, swivel from the waist to follow the car for a good fifty yards before you will want to press the shutter, and equalize your camera movement so that it moves at the same relative speed as the car. (The sharpness won't be good if you pan faster or slower than the car is moving.)

When the car passes through your point of focus (preferably at a right angle to you), press the shutter gently, so you don't generate camera movement, *then continue following the car,* by still swivelling from the waist, for another twenty yards or so after you've taken the photo to complete the follow-through. Just like a golfer or a tennis player, your follow-through has a decided effect on your result.

If your panning is very smooth but you are getting vertical movement, then the car probably is in a bumpy area of the circuit. If you know in advance that the track is bumpy there, but that is the only place you have to shoot the pan shot, then raise your shutter speed up a stop and you should stop the vertical movement. However, you will lose the blurring of the background and freeze the tires a little bit more, too.

On the other hand, sometimes you might want to *increase* the vertical movement, lowering the shutter speed one or even two or three stops to generate more vertical camera movement for a special effect. But remember, the tires should always appear to be in motion, with the wheels spinning and the white letters on the side at least partially blurred; that shows movement. The only completely stopped tires should be on parked cars!

Panning involves lots of variables and requires a lot of practice to perfect. Some of those variables include the choice of lens, the car's speed, and the surface smoothness of the track, as well as your ability to focus accurately—not to mention keeping the camera steady and pressing the shutter smoothly at the right time! Keeping the camera steady (all of the time) and pressing the shutter gently are the first priorities for good, consistent results.

You can achieve steadiness—at the expense of mobility and a fluid follow-through—by using a tripod. There's a time and a place for them, too, but in racing photography with a 35mm you want to stay spontaneous, and tripods inhibit spontaneity.

Peak action and repetition must be watched carefully. Most cars and drivers behave in the same way lap after lap and tend to be in just about the same position every lap. Watch these cars and drivers carefully; see what they are doing (lifting wheels, jumping over bumps, bottoming out, oversteering, or sparking when they bottom out). See if they do it consistently, and capture it the next time around.

Wait for the peak of the action, that little—but significant—pause or hesitation between the suspension's full extension and return; there is a millisecond where all motion stops, freezes, and waits to go the other direction. This movement can be vertical or horizontal, but there is a point in time that action stops, hesitates, and then reverses its course; it's all a matter of physics and inertia. When this tiny moment occurs, this instant of suspended motion, then press your shutter (gently, gently!) and your photos will have more excitement.

The best techniques are developed by practice, success and failure, trial and error. You learn what works best for you. *Action is action*, and you can practice shooting action anywhere—the streets, the highway, or even the horse-racing track. The more you practice shooting action, the better you will get. So practice!

For the start of the race as well as for the finish (the overdone, trite, checkered-flag shot), I prefer to shoot at a higher shutter speed to completely freeze the action. If there is action or drama at the start or finish, you will want to record it as sharply as possible. For the start of a race, usually 1/500 will be fast enough, but 1/1000 may be even better. Anticipating the possible action, use a medium-to-long telephoto lens, and try to catch the cars turning across the frame, not just head-on. If they are just coming head-on, a lower shutter speed will be adequate, but as they pass across the diagonal of the frame they will blur unless you use a higher shutter speed. And since you have very little control over the drivers, you have to be ready for them to suddenly veer across on a diagonal!

For the checkered flag I generally prefer to shoot at a thousandth of a second, as it is usually shot with long telephoto (300mm to 600mm) or with a wide-angle (15mm to 20mm). In both cases you usually want to stop all the motion to capture the drama: the finish line, the checkered flag and the winner's gesture, or the closeness of victory. This usually requires a higher shutter speed. Usually you want to create the illusion of motion in order to capture the feeling of speed, but in this case you want to freeze it in order to capture the drama of the moment.

Still, there must be some element of motion, or *anticipated* motion, in the frame of the photograph to create excitement (the checkered flag waving, the shadow of the flag, the cheering of the team, or the gesture of the driver: all are good places to start). The photo must be sharp and frozen, yet still provide the illusion of speed to provide the drama of the race.

## CHAPTER 8: SPECIAL TECHNIQUES

This chapter covers a lot of loose ends that can make your photographs just a bit snappier than those of the guy next to you.

One of the easiest techniques to try is the "zoom shot." This causes a blur of color, radiating from the center to the outside edges of the photograph or from the outside to the center. It will enhance the feeling of speed, but it can become quite boring if overdone. It can be described as a burst of color!

The best lens for a zoom shot is probably an 80-200. The procedure is simple: set your shutter speed to 1/8, 1/15, or 1/30; focus on a subject (or wait for it to reach your pre-focus zone), and zoom the lens *while you are making the exposure.* Don't forget to set the f-stop to correspond with the shutter speed.

The mechanical element of the zoom shot is easily mastered, but the results are mixed. It is dependent upon a lot of variables: subject speed, shutter speed, choice of lens, and how fast and how smoothly you zoom the lens.

I prefer the push-pull type of zoom lenses for these shots, as opposed to the ones with rotating zooming rings, because the latter tend to add camera movement. The zoom can be done either pushing or pulling, whichever works best for you.

These are perfect techniques to use Kodachrome 25. It works very well for the zoom shot, as anything much over 64 ISO will be too fast to allow for the ultra-small apertures you need. On a day with full sun, using Kodachrome 25, your f-stop will be f22 at 1/15 of a second—so forget about a film as fast as 400 ISO!

If the weather is slightly overcast, or even very dark, other films will work, too, but watch your exposure and be sure that your film speed is within the usable range of your camera and lens for these techniques.

Another artistic technique that works quite effectively is the use of very slow shutter speeds. These emphasize horizontal movement, vertical movement, and camera movement. It helps to be close to your subject, too; a wide-angle lens, or even a 50mm normal lens, will work out best for this one.

You will want to use a shutter speed of 1/8, 1/15 or 1/30 of a second. Remember, the slower the shutter speed, the more movement you will create. If you pan with your subject during the exposure, the movement will be more than just a blur across the frame. Move with your subject, try some even slower exposures, maybe 1/2 or even a whole second—see what happens!

The use of filters for special effects is virtually limitless. You can get filters for starburst effects and speed lines, toned filters for sky, multiimage filters, and many more. Each filter has a lot of possibilities that extend past the obvious. Experiment, play with them, practice to see what works best for you. You may want to combine a few filters for something really different. There are lots of options.

A filter that I like a lot is the speed filter; the results can vary considerably, depending on how it is used. I prefer a 1/125 shutter speed to keep the background blurred if photographing a moving car; there is nothing more disconcerting than seeing half a car stopped, with background and tires frozen, while the other half of the car is just a blur of speed lines and color.

A lens that works well with this filter is an 80-200 zoom, usually using about the 100mm range. Interesting effects can be achieved with helmets and other still subjects, too. The speed lines change with filter rotation. Have some fun—play with it.

Try some other filters, too. Cokin® makes a great variety of filters of very high quality that will fill most of your needs. Just make sure that all your shots don't start looking alike; don't get stuck doing the same thing all the time just because it works. Experiment!

Combining flash and available light can give some pretty interesting results; the darker the scene range, the better your results should be. With Kodachrome 25 on a really dark day, the combination of flash and natural light can really pop.

With this technique I prefer to set the flash on manual. Your lens choice can be wide-angle, a normal lens (50-70mm), or a short telephoto, depending on how much of the car you want on your film. This is another technique of trial and error, test and experiment.

Depending on when your camera's flash triggers (that is, at the begining or the end of your shutter opening), you will get different results. One result will be a fixed image with a blur leading to it, if your flash is triggered at the start of the exposure. If your flash is triggered at the end of the the exposure, then you will have a fixed image with a blur trailing away from it. In both cases you will want to pan during the exposure.

As for the exposure if you are in full sun, let's use Kodachrome 25; set your lens at f22 with an exposure of 1/15 of a second. Set your ISO on the flash to 50, and expose normally with the flash turned on.

If you are in dark conditions, shadow or overcast, you might want to stick with Kodachrome 64. Take your light reading as normal, but set your flash to reflect an ISO number one stop higher (ISO 125), so you are simply using the flash as a fill augmenting the available light.

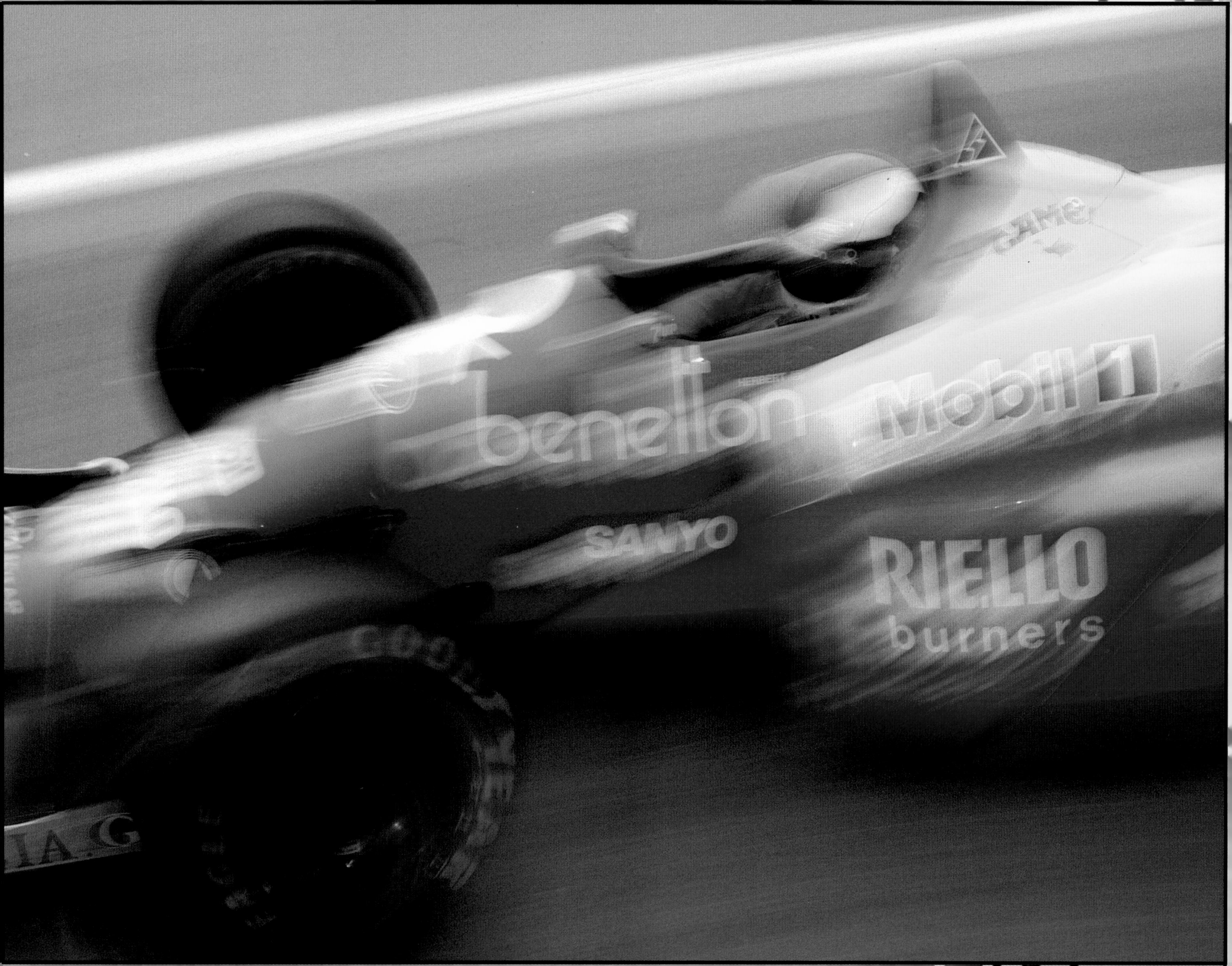
benetton
Mobil 1
SANYO
RIELLO
burners

There are a lot of special techniques, such as multiple exposures, in which the success rate is not very high nor is the consistency. Any special effect will require a lot of practice and luck, and you'll see some failure, too; but don't give up, keep trying. That's how new photographic looks are developed.

You might shoot two or three rolls trying to get a multiple exposure right, and you might only get one image out of all of that film that is really good—but it's worth it!

There are still a lot of things that haven't been done, so look for them. Try some things that were done a long time ago but forgotten or not fully explored, like Kodak Ektachrome infra-red color film—it can be a lot of fun. Try using a yellow filter with it and you'll get rid of a lot of the purple, but the reds will go Porsche yellow while the organic greens go red—and they really pop!

Try this (and all special techniques) as a supplement to whatever else you want to do, or you just might wind up without anything at all that you can use. Be careful that you don't use any special technique so often that all your photos look the same; give your photos a good mix. Just because one thing works well, don't get stuck doing only that. Be adventurous, think, take some creative chances; they just might work. Don't be discouraged if they don't work the first time, or the first several times—just keep trying. Experiment!

## CHAPTER 9: ADVERSE CONDITIONS

Get out in the rain; that's one of the best times to get movement and color. The possibilities of color and movement are limitless. You could create a photo essay on just reflections and water drops. The most important thing is to keep your film and the inside of the camera dry during a film change. Electronic cameras have some advantages, but most will self destruct in the rain; a good old mechanical-type camera will keep plugging away. Just make sure you keep the inside of the camera (and the film you are loading into it) *dry*, or it will jam when the film sticks to itself.

One of the best tools to keep everything dry is a poncho. You can go inside them to change your film, and they keep you and your cameras dry, but a poncho doesn't allow the cameras to heat up as they do inside a coat. The difference in temperature is important; if you keep your cameras inside your coat they might stay dry, but they will be a different temperature than the outside atmosphere, and you will have a very serious problem of fogging glass and condensation, sometimes even inside the camera and on your film. It is definitely best to keep the camera the same temperature as your shooting location. The same can be said for taking a camera straight out of a warm car to shoot in the cold: *Pow! Fog!*

When it starts raining, many photographers pack it up and head for shelter, but some of the most dramatic and beautiful shots come with the rain. Colors, movement and reflections really jump out at you, especially if the sun comes out full after a rain squall. It's definitely one of the most beautiful times to photograph racing cars.

A rainy day is an excellent time to try out slow shutter speeds in order to "paint" colors of movement. Oddly enough, you will have more light on a dark day if it is raining than if it is just overcast. I really don't like shooting in the overcast, as the colors don't jump as well, but a simple 81B or 81C filter will relieve some of the blue hue to the overcast scene. They are also useful in adding a little warmth to a shaded scene.

You will learn different techniques in adverse conditions, those that work best for you; the main thing is to protect your film first and your camera second. The other real danger is dust and sand. At a really windy circuit there is usually an abundance of dust or sand, fine sand. Be extra careful; make every effort, during loading, to keep the film plane free of dust or sand, and clean your cameras carefully at the end of the day. One neglected grain of sand in your camera can ruin a whole roll of film or more!

## CHAPTER 10:  PHYSICAL DANGERS

If you are photographing trackside, be careful! It is really dangerous. Just because you have a guardrail between you and the cars doesn't mean that they can't come off the track, plunge over or through the guard rail, and hit you. A crash may send bits of the car flying in your direction—bits and pieces that can kill you.

Keep your head and arms on your own side of the guardrail; don't lean out of photo windows or hang out over the rail. (What you hang out there you just might lose!) Never let your camera strap hang down over the track; a wing might catch it as the car passes by just under it, and straps have been known to break or mysteriously detach themselves, always at the worst possible times. Remember, a camera is heavy, and if it hits the car or the driver it is going to do some massive damage!

Be safe, not sorry. Think! It is better not to even lean against the guardrail, even if you think you are in a safe position. I've seen legs broken by a car that hit the guardrail fifteen feet from the person leaning on it; the steel bends sends out shock waves, creating an oscillation that will affect it much further down the rail than the point of impact. Be careful; try to leave about a six-inch gap between your body and the rail.

Watch what is happening all of the time. Pay attention. Watch where the cars are coming from. Make it a practice to walk so that the cars are coming toward you as you go around the circuit; it gives you an opportunity to see what they are doing if they get into a problem. Always listen for the odd noise of the motor or tires; that can give you some warning that there is a problem.

When an accident happens, it is incredibly quick, and sometimes you only have a split second to decide where to go. You had better be right! In most instances it is safest to run toward where the car has already been, not away from it, as usually the car or its pieces will follow you if you backpedal. Remember the physics of the situation: The car or former pieces of it will continue in a straight line until their energy is spent—and a ten-pound hunk of debris travelling a hundred miles an hour packs a lot of energy.

Don't turn your back on the oncoming traffic following an incident; you must be able to see what the cars are doing at all times. Remember, more cars will be arriving at an accident scene, often compounding the danger. If you have to reload or are looking for something in your camera case while in a dangerous position and can't concentrate on what the cars are doing, move to a safer spot until you are again ready to take photos and can concentrate on what's going on around you.

## CHAPTER 11: A SPECIAL EYE

Try to look at things differently than everyone else, through your own eye. Don't try to copy, try to *create*. Take photographic risks; maybe it'll work, maybe it won't, but you don't know till you try. If it works, you've created a photo that's different and special. Try the extraordinary; use creative angles and different lenses; approach a subject in a different manner than normal.

Don't just concentrate on the cars—boring! Add some color, something that tells the viewer where you are. Rio for example: Wow! What a place! What color! Maybe a samba show. Maybe the sunbathers on the Copacabana! Maybe the mechanics taking a break playing soccer. Maybe a taxi ride to the circuit. Who knows? The possibilities are limitless.

Use your perception to enhance the subject and make the photograph contain your own creative difference. Look for different shapes, visual movement, or maybe a repetition of shapes and colors, like nose cones or rear wings. Find *textures*, the balance of coarse and fine, heavy and soft-toned. Think of the contrast of mechanics' hands and drivers' hands. Make the subject a part of its surroundings—or make it alienated from them and completely out of place. Use *your eyes*—but most important of all, use *your mind*. Think! Conceptualize and *visualize!*

Have fun. Bring back lots of fantastic photos. Practice! Practice! Practice! You really *will* get better, so don't get discouraged; but remember, motor racing is a dangerous sport, and there are real physical risks for all concerned. Don't take any chances that could not only endanger yourself, but the drivers, the spectators, or the sport itself.

Drink
Coca
GOODYEAR
GOODYEAR
Drink
ALBORETO
R.ARNOUX
Agip
Marlboro
Marlboro

All text, photography, layout, and design by John Blakemore. Printing by Lithotone, Indianapolis, Indiana, under the direction of Jim Priebe. Color separations by In & Out Litho Plate, Los Angeles, California, overseen by Athena Ubach. Binding by Steve Muchmore, the National Bindery of Pomona, California. Layout and design were done on an Apple Macintosh SE using Microsoft Word and Aldus PageMaker. Typesetting directed by Shiraz Januwala, on a Linotronic 300 by Krishna Copy Center, Berkeley California. All photographs were done with Nikon or Canon cameras using Kodachrome film exclusively.

Special thanks to: Alain Prost; Bernard Bakalian; Jean-louis Moncet; Satch Carlson;John Bisignano and Ryder Houston of Performance Marketing; Marilyn Stefonetti and Refractions camera store, Albany, California; Jan Livingston; Lewis & Lewis Computers, Anchorage, Alaska; Mike Kranfuss and the Ford Motor Company; Jean-Jacques Delaruwiere and Renault Sport; Duncan Lee and R.J. Reynolds; Agnes Carlier and Philip Morris; Road and Track magazine; Garvin Brown; John Delayre; Bob Fritsky; Patricia Gentz; George Goad; Terry Griffin; Robert Hough; Keith Hudak; Mark Karp; Pamela Lauesen; Elaine Medoff; Catherine Metral; Mary Randall; Barry Simpson; and Bruce Trenery.